R...

Tea...

THE GOLDEN

Rock T-...

Editor: Tamar Brazis
Designer: Becky Terhune
Production Manager: Kaija Markoe

Library of Congress Cataloging-in-Publication Data has been applied for.
ISBN 10: 0-8109-7053-8
ISBN 13: 978-1-8109-7053-3

Printed and bound in China
10 9 8 7 6 5 4 3 2 1

HNA ▌▌▌▌▌
harry n. abrams, inc.
a subsidiary of La Martinière Groupe
115 West 18th Street
New York, NY 10011
www.hnabooks.com

Rock Tease

THE GOLDEN YEARS OF Rock T-Shirts

Erica Easley & Ed Chalfa

Abrams Image
New York

Contents

Introduction
Rock Tease it's called, and a rock tease it is.

This book is not an encyclopedia of rock T-shirts. A viable book with those intentions would be as thick as the *Oxford English Dictionary*—too heavy (and too expensive) to be enjoyed. Rather, this book is a teaser—a selection of some of the best rock T-shirts produced over a twenty-five-year period: 1970—1995. These are the golden years of rock T-shirts, the period during which they transformed from limited-run band and crew swag, to hip souvenirs printed up by savvy entrepreneurs and, finally, to a major socio-fashion phenomenon. The shirts presented on the following pages represent only a fraction of the total number of rock tees manufactured during that time, but they reflect the evolution in design and industry, which has kept rock shirts popular through the ages. Of course, some very notable, fabulous artists are not represented: New York Dolls, Slade, Soundgarden. . . . Going through a list of important rock-and-roll acts not featured by tees in this book, it would be easy to claim that some major artists have been omitted.

But rock T-shirts aren't just time-capsule souvenirs. They are art. They are product. They are clothing meant to be worn and worn-out. It's impossible to estimate how many rock T-shirts were produced during the period between 1970 and 1995, and there is no way of knowing what percentage of these vintage shirts is still with us. Washing, wear, and time take their toll on all forms of clothing, not least of all T-shirts. Unarguably, the majority of classic rock tees has been lost to disintegration via frequent wearing or car waxing, or to Goodwill donation bins due to changing tastes.

It is also important to remember that rock shirts were a nascent industry in the 1970s (and all but nonexistent in the '60s), so many favorite bands from back in the day never even had promotional T-shirts during their original periods of success. (As proof of this point, while working on this book we were fortunate enough to connect with Angela Davis, head of Svengirly, a music management company and, among other things, the person in charge of licensing the band T. Rex—on behalf of Marc Bolan's son, Rolan—in the U.S.A. In early discussions about the rock T-shirt industry, we learned from Davis that Rolan thought the first shirts produced celebrating his father dated back to 1976. During the writing of this book, however, we discovered pictures of Iggy Pop hanging out with Lou Reed and David Bowie in

1972—and wearing a T.Rex T-shirt! It just goes to show how little is really known about this undocumented industry.) The reality is, due to the organic effects of time and the development of the rock shirt phenomenon, many great rock groups are not "adequately represented" in vintage T-shirts.

But then again, *Rock Tease* does not aspire to be a novel approach to the history of rock and roll, so making any broad presumptions about shirts included (or excluded) in this book misses the point. As symbiotic as the relationship between the tees and the music may be, the inspiration for this book was and remains the artistry and social significance of the rock T-shirts themselves. The cachet of rock tees has always been their aura of insider status, their je ne sais quoi of coolness that could not be created by a logo alone. Though it is impossible, as well as inappropriate, to remove the significance of the music from the shirts, it is likewise shortsighted to think that the only value of these tees is promotional.

That said, unlike the celebrated art of concert posters and album covers, critics have not yet given the artistry of vintage rock T-shirts much consideration. Both as products and as an industry, rock shirts are wholly undocumented. Many rock-and-roll collectibles dealers, as well as major auction houses with pop culture departments, like Sotheby's and Christie's, do not work with vintage rock shirts. (The exception to this unofficial rule might be rare, early T-shirts for major artists like Elvis Presley and the Beatles, who were heavily licensed during the first waves of their careers—anomalies for music artists of their eras.) Yet, over the past five or so years, the prices for vintage rock tees have risen dramatically. Vintage retailers and online sellers routinely get hundreds, even thousands of dollars for authentic rock shirts. Clearly, a lack of critical recognition has in no way dampened the public's enthusiasm for a great, old rock T-shirt. Rock T-shirts are our culture.

Indeed, rock tees are an integral part of the rock-and-roll experience. Bought and worn by millions of fans, rock tees defined who was cool—and why. They were, at one time, cheap souvenirs, but their imagery has become a major influence on the way we think about and experience music and, as fans, how we relate to each other. During the innovative twenty-five-year period covered in *Rock Tease*, rock T-shirt design boldly developed, and also promoted, enduring rock iconography. Today, these tees are icons in their own right.

One of the most egregious assumptions about rock T-shirt graphics holds that they are simply low-budget screen prints of album cover art. Sure, some shirts do feature rehashed album images, but the majority of rock tees produced between 1970 and 1995 showcase original graphics that reflect the changing values and aesthetics of rock and roll. There is an obvious evolution in the art of rock tees, its execution and its themes, as well as in the basic styles of the shirts themselves. Thus, *Rock Tease* is arranged by decade to highlight the overlooked era-specific trends of rock T-shirt design—how the literalism and simplicity of '70s rock shirts gave way to grandiose designs in the '80s, or how the early '70s representation of guitar legend Jimi Hendrix compares with that of '80s virtuoso Jake E. Lee. Just consider the difference between the early '70s Aerosmith tee featured on page 19 with the '80s Aerosmith T-shirt on page 78: The early shirt is a crude, small, single-color print of the band's logo, while the later shirt features a dynamic multicolor print of an exploding stadium, fleeing crowd, and bold band logo across the front.

Viewed in this manner, it is also easy to see the medium's diversity. After all, the best rock T-shirt designs convey the founding tenets of rock and roll—sex, power, rebellion, cool—then add flourishes corresponding to the promoted artist's unique look and sound. Seventies Jethro Tull T-shirts, for instance, regularly feature castles, flowers, and flutes—Renaissance-style imagery that isn't specific to rock and roll but which complements the band's fantasy-inspired music. Likewise, an L.A. Guns tee from their 1988 tour pairs a riff on the group's detailed guns-and-badge logo with illustrations of tattooed chicks in high heels—perfectly representing the bad-boy sex, drugs, and rock-and-roll Sunset Strip-metal subculture of which L.A. Guns was a prominent fixture. And in the early '90s, when it seemed like everything that could possibly be done with rock T-shirts had already been explored, grunge artists made their T-shirts interesting and appropriate by styling rock tees that deviated 180 degrees from those of earlier decades: Whereas '70s and '80s tees tended to be small and fitted, often with bright accent colors and intricate designs, '90s rock designs rejected that look with oversized shirts, drapey fits, and subdued, minimalist graphics.

Even if you look at tees from a single era in rock, there is an impressive variety of design approaches. Take the mid-'80s peak of heavy metal, a phase in rock and roll commonly derided as lacking in substance and originality. Rock T-shirts from this time tell a different story. Viewed as a group, these shirts show an obvious departure from the tees of late '70s top rockers—a clear indication that the music was going in a new direction. It's important to note how the artistry of heavy metal tees moves away from design techniques used on classic rock tees to distance the bands from what came before them. Metal's T-shirts are loaded with color and usually feature a prominent central graphic. Thanks to these changes, they have an in-your-face impact that echoes the music's angry, antisocial drift. But T-shirts for different artists within the genre still vary noticeably. The shirts for Mötley Crüe, one of metal's biggest stars, never depict the band performing (unlike tees for early acts like Journey or the Who) but instead often feature a group pose, emphasizing that the Crüe is a gang—a social force—more than just a band. Early Crüe shirts have touches of devil worship, while later T-shirts favor motorcycles and bimbos as means of establishing the group's rowdy-marauder reputation. Conversely, tees for W.A.S.P., another big metal act, don't tap into the sexual and mischievous so overtly. W.A.S.P., musically, is more vulgar and even campier than Mötley Crüe so, not surprisingly, the imagery on their T-shirts is more apocalyptic, incorporating animal skulls, bones, rocks, and blood. It is tough guy—meets—Dungeons and Dragons.

As it turns out, the best rock tees aren't just promotional schlock of a static format. Rather, they are like pop culture folk art. Rock T-shirts are readable, recognizable symbols for masses of rock fans; their graphics typify the way we think about the music. Blending the zeitgeist of rock and roll with the values and sensibilities of a particular artist, great rock shirts create a uniquely cool presence.

But, of course, because we put them on our bodies, the art of rock T-shirts is as important in self-promotion as it is in artist promotion. Peers read rock shirts the way CEOs review resumes—as a quick rundown of all you are about. Such is the influence and impact of rock and roll that wearing a rock tee not only announces to the world what you think is cool, it announces that *you* are cool, too! Donning a rock T-shirt suggests that you not only identify with the sound and image of a given artist, but that you identify through that artist. Wear an Ozzy Osbourne—era Black Sabbath T-shirt, and your peers know you are dark and intense. Put on a David Lee Roth—era Van Halen tee, and others get the message that you are into rock music for wild, good times. The images on your shirt, as much as the name, reflect what you are about and where you want to be.

Adding a layer to that idea is the resurgent popularity of vintage rock T-shirts and the booming reproduction rock tee market. Today, vintage rock shirts aren't just worn by nostalgic baby boomers and aging punks—the audiences which first appreciated them. Many of the people driving the explosive vintage rock T-shirt market are folks in their teens and twenties. And these are the same consumers snapping up reproduction rock T-shirts—newly manufactured tees that feature vintage rock tee graphics reprinted on retro-style T-shirts. Though there are certainly numerous reasons why anyone wears a particular rock tee, the clamor for the look of classic rock tees, like those featured in this book, is proof that the appeal of rock shirts extends beyond a core music audience. It's no longer about wearing the shirt as proof you went to the concert. Rock T-shirts have become the centerpiece of rock-and-roll style, an American fashion statement on par with jeans and sneakers.

Perhaps it is precisely because rock tees were not made with an eye to posterity that they have held up so well—they were designed for immediate gratification, and that immediacy is still palpable in the imagery today. Vintage rock T-shirts don't have to strive to represent what makes rock and roll exciting and inspiring; they were there as it happened. In fact, they helped it happen. The energy, the creativity, the camaraderie, the fashion, the celebration, the sex, the drugs, the theatrics, the music: Everything you need to know about rock and roll is writ large on rock T-shirts.

Born in the U.S.A.: A Brief Pre-History to the Dawn of Rock T-Shirts

In 1956, Elvis Presley became the world's first rock star. It only makes sense that he would have the world's first rock T-shirt.

Interesting enough, the first Elvis tee was printed up by one of the singer's fan clubs—not by any of the numerous companies that licensed his name or image. Fifty years before J.Lo, Elvis Presley had one of the most impressive endorsement and merchandise empires in entertainment history, featuring everything from lipsticks to plastic toy guitars. But no T-shirts.

At the time Elvis first rose to fame in the mid '50s, cotton T-shirts were still regarded strictly as men's underwear (a role they had popularly filled since they were invented in the early twentieth century). Women did not wear them, period. And very few men would dare to wear them as anything *but* an undershirt. Marlon Brando and James Dean shocked the era's movie audiences when their fringe culture characters donned white tees as outerwear in the classic films *The Wild One* (1954) and *Rebel Without A Cause* (1955), respectively. T-shirts, even blank ones, were anything but a regular fashion statement.

But the rebel icons of the '50s had let the shirt out of the bag—so to speak—and by the late '60s, tees were becoming part of mainstream fashion. Once the public accepted their favorite screen idols in T-shirts, it wasn't long before business innovators started exploring the promotional possibilities of tees. An ongoing cultural revolution and advancements in printing technology (most notably the invention of Plastisol, a durable, fabric ink introduced in 1959), allowed for increased experimentation with the T-shirt medium throughout the decade. While the earliest printed T-shirts date only to the mid 1940s, by the end of the '60s, printed tees were increasingly common; business entities from Disney to Budweiser were manufacturing promotional T-shirts.

At the same time T-shirts were coming into their own, rock and roll was emerging as a major and enduring social force. At the end of the 1960s, there were several notable "scenes," including the British Invasion (the Beatles, the Rolling Stones), psychedelic San Francisco (the Grateful Dead, Jefferson Airplane), and Los Angeles's Sunset Strip (the Doors, the Byrds). Rock bands appeared on TV and in magazines. They had fan clubs and fanzines.

And, in Bill Graham, rock music had its first modern, visionary promoter. Graham started in San Francisco, not so much as a fan of the rock scene, but as an insightful entrepreneur who recognized that rock and roll could be a business as much as an art form. By the end of the '60s, he owned and managed the key rock-and-roll concert venues Fillmore West (in San Francisco) and Fillmore East (in New York City). Everybody who was anybody, or wanted to be somebody, played at the Fillmores. Graham's roster of print artists developed the poster art which came to define the psychedelic movement. At the tail end of 1968, Graham began printing up T-shirts to commemorate the shows at his clubs.

Bill Graham was most likely the first person to print rock tees on a regular basis, as well as the first serious businessman to consider the idea of a "rock T-shirt" independent of a major merchandising effort. (Beatles tees were printed as early as 1964, but they coincided with other branded products, including Beatles bobble heads and sneakers. The T-shirts were hardly a stand-alone enterprise.) Graham's late-'60s tees celebrate the major San Francisco artists who were regulars at his west coast venue with simple designs. For instance, a 1968 New Year's concert shirt features "Jefferson Airplane" in block letters over a basic peace symbol. (This shirt and others from the Graham archive can be viewed at www.wolfgangsvault.com.)

While Graham was cutting-edge among the music establishment, his initial forays into rock T-shirts corresponded with early bootlegging (production of unsanctioned shirts for sale at events). By way of comparison, in 1969 Woodstock promoters organized a milestone three-day festival of top '60s rockers—from Jimi Hendrix to Sly and the Family Stone, Janis Joplin to Alvin Lee—and printed up T-shirts to memorialize the event: ten of them. They were given only as mementos to their senior staff. Anticipated attendance at Woodstock was about 60,000; actual attendance exceeded 400,000. Yet, while the event promoters did not foresee the possibilities of concert T-shirt sales, streetwise hippies did. One attendee of the festival, Jim Swofford, reported to *The Cincinnati Enquirer* that he bought his beloved Woodstock logo tee out of the back of a Volkswagen bus on the New York State Thruway en route to the concert—for five dollars. The times, they were indeed a changin'. Rock T-shirts had arrived.

High Time: Rock

In the 1970s, the late-'60s T-shirt innovation of concert promoter Bill Graham and rock scene opportunists truly took hold, creating an era which should officially be recognized as the first decade of rock T-shirts. Over this tumultuous ten-year period, rock shirts went from scattered anomalies to a major force in the business of rock and roll; from an item given gratis to the band, crew, and record execs, to a product available for purchase at concerts and head shops across the country. It was the decade that most shaped the icon.

Central to the rise of rock T-shirts at this time was a social shift occurring outside of the music industry—the '70s transformation of T-shirts from a fringe fashion statement to a popular everyday garment for both men and women. The increased acceptance of T-shirts resulted in not only a greater, more accessible supply of cheap, blank T-shirts, but also more businesses equipped to print them. Consequently, in the early '70s, it was relatively easy for anyone with the inclination to start printing up tees.

Not surprising, the increased opportunity for making T-shirts, paired with a hungry and growing rock-and-roll audience, floated dollar signs before the eyes of many aspiring entrepreneurs and created a free-for-all business environment that dominated most of the decade. The situation was compounded by the novelty of merchandising opportunities for most recording artists; licensing was a non-issue for nearly all performers before the '70s. Thus, there was absolutely nothing to stop Joe Schmoe from taking a band's name or image and sticking it on a T-shirt, to be sold for his personal profit. Though T-shirts made in this manner would come to be known as bootlegs (unauthorized products), the reality is that most rock shirts from the first half of the decade are of this origin.

Rock tee graphics from the early '70s clearly reflect this primitive start. Take for instance, the Byrds' tee, circa 1970, on page 14. It is a single-color print, front graphic only, with no indication of its date or place of origin. This is the case, too, with other early-'70s shirts featured on the following pages: David Bowie, Jimi Hendrix, Lou Reed . . . they each showcase basic (even crude) graphics and simple printing techniques. Most likely, these T-shirts were made in limited runs for sale at a head shop or concert parking lot.

Tees in the 1970s

Of course, as the '70s wore on and rock T-shirts became an increasingly lucrative product, escalating competition drove design and industry innovations. By the middle of the decade, dating shirts to a specific tour or album was becoming increasingly popular. The earliest shirt in this book representing that trend is a bootleg 1975 Rolling Stones tour tee on page 21 (the Stones were one of the first groups to have official tour shirts, as early as 1972). The shirt is actually a double-whammy because it also notes the concert location—New York City.

It was also in the mid '70s that Bill Graham launched the first music merchandising company, Winterland Productions, with Dave and Dell Furano. The revolutionary business was an immediate success; by 1977 the company that was started in the coatroom of Graham's San Francisco concert hall (Winterland Ballroom) was making between twelve and fourteen million dollars annually on the sale of rock tees. As the first major company to organize within the cutthroat rock T-shirt market, Winterland set the standard in business practices—most significantly, by pursuing licensing rights from artists through the end of the '70s and into the next decade.

Overall, the graphics of '70s rock T-shirts are most distinguished by what might best be called their sincerity. Though many images, particularly from the first half of the decade, seem unsophisticated, the artwork is firmly grounded in a realistic representation of the performer. Interestingly, many of the shirts which flaunt illustrations of the artist depict them performing—singing, playing guitar—highlighting just what the shirt is about. At the same time, there are no touches of whimsy or fantasy, no portrayals of an artist as larger than life, or promotion of peripheral themes. The designs on '70s rock tees were tied very strictly to the existing images and reputations of the artist, imbuing the shirts with an earnestness and individuality that remains poignant thirty years later.

Few rock tees this old still look this good. It's a perfect example of a single-color printing,
front-graphic-only tee with a straightforward homage to the artist.

The Byrds ca. 1970

Simple, hand-drawn illustrations are hallmarks of great early-'70s tees. This one is particularly special for its four-color printing, which is uncommon in early rock shirts.

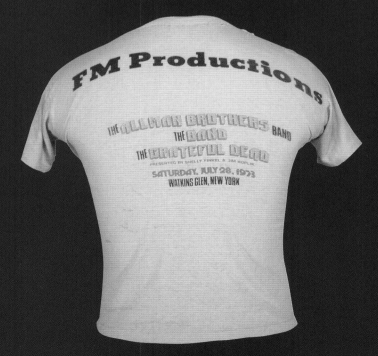

Watkins Glen Festival *1973*

A crudely printed portrait of a musical legend, this shirt is an example of those made in limited runs and sold in head shops or parking lots.

Jimi Hendrix *ca. 1973*

Illustrated portraits are typical graphics for '70s rock tees. The images are unsophisticated, reflecting the grassroots origin of the rock T-shirt business. By the early '80s, the industry would be dominated by major merchandising companies, and primitive tees, like these for David Bowie, Lou Reed, or Jimi Hendrix (previous page), would already seem antiquated.

David Bowie *ca. 1973*
Lou Reed *ca. 1974*

Early logo tees for legendary artists—they seem quite simple and understated now; they are regarded as classics.

Aerosmith ca. 1974
KISS 1974

An example of album art being put on a tee—and creating a whole new impression. The giant eyes are gripping.

Sweet 1976

An early Winterland Productions T-shirt (above), shows a distinctive approach to touting Frampton's British roots—with symbols of pedigree. The Manhattan skyline on this bootleg T-shirt (below) makes it extremely collectible, even among the most rare Stones shirts. While listing a venue or city was not uncommon for vintage tour tees, the graphic representation of a specific location was very unique because it rendered an entire design worthless after one concert.

Peter Frampton *1976*
The Rolling Stones *1975*

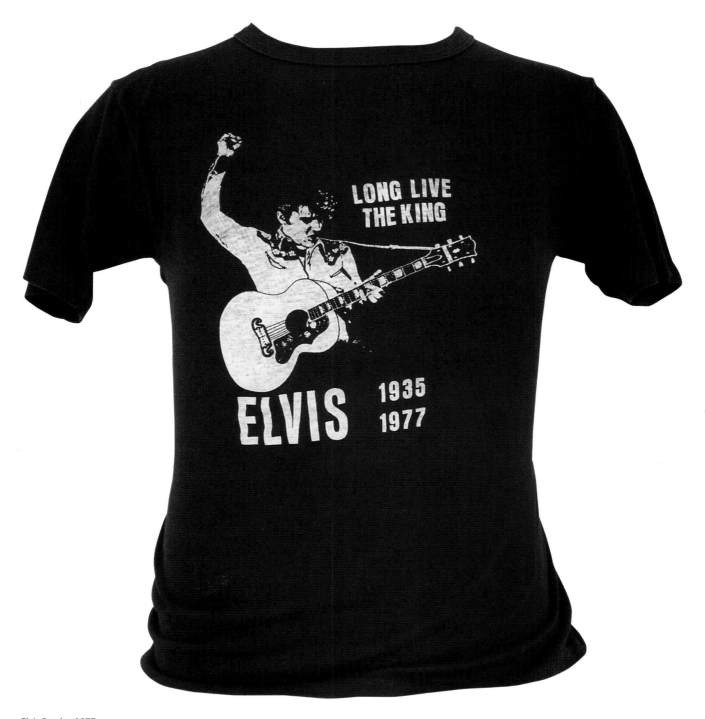

Elvis Presley *1977*

Two examples of bootleg shirts made to memorialize the King's passing. The shirt on the opposite page has a classic simplicity, fitting for rock's original superstar, while the shirt on this page is endearing for its devoted amateurism.

Elvis Presley *1977*

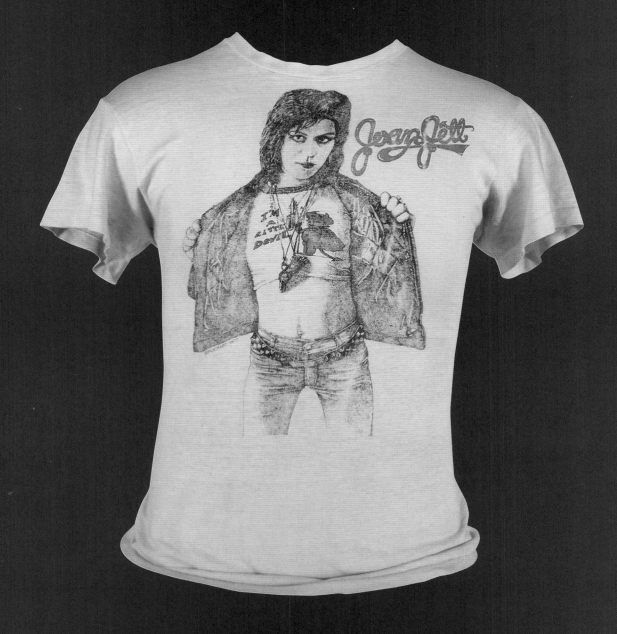

This meticulously illustrated T-shirt for teenage Joan Jett (made while she was still in the Runaways!) is a testament to the devotion of her cult following. The picture of Joan staring out at you gives this tee a particularly powerful, reverent vibe.

Joan Jett *1977*

By the late '70s, four-color T-shirts were increasingly common. These bootleg tees employ color to great effect, using it to highlight the energy conveyed in the performance-oriented graphics.

Jethro Tull *1977*
Led Zeppelin *1977*

Styx 1977

By the later '70s, rock was clearly splintering into sub-genres, as these tees for prog rock groups Styx (opposite), and Emerson, Lake & Palmer (above) prove. The intellectual tone of their graphics is a sure indication that these artists are not in sync with the raw power represented on the T-shirts of, say, punk star Iggy Pop (next page).

Emerson, Lake & Palmer *1977*

IGGY SAID IT.
IGGY HAD
THE POWER
IGGY HAD
THE
DISEASE

With so many images of a single performer crowding the shirt, this Iggy Pop amateur bootleg is a design anomaly that would never be confused with a professionally designed shirt. As a result, it's an exceptional reflection of Iggy's then-underground punk appeal.

Iggy Pop ca. 1977

A very witty design appropriation makes maximum use of single-color printing.
Lynyrd Skynyrd + Jack Daniel's = sex, drugs, and southern rock and roll!

Lynyrd Skynyrd *1977*

This T-shirt was given out with the press kit for the Sex Pistols' debut album, *Never Mind the Bollocks, Here's the Sex Pistols*; it is by far the smartest, best rock tee made by a record label to tout a record release (corporate involvement usually led to watered-down graphics). Though the print on both sides is simply the recognizable album art, look closely at the back side of the shirt. The tag is on the outside! These tees were intentionally printed inside out, a little detail that reflects just how conceptually genius and deviant the Sex Pistols' camp was.

Sex Pistols *1977*

By the late '70s, one of the biggest changes in rock T-shirts was the sudden prevalence of printing on black shirts. Though various colored tees would still appear, black quickly became the dominant rock T-shirt color—at least in part because it maintained rock's tough, dangerous image. The crooked graphics common to bootleg T-shirts are a good reminder of the industry's ragtag history. The fact that fans tolerated oddly off-center prints—that they would even wear imperfection for the sake of the band—highlights the tremendous social significance of these tees.

California Jam Festival ca.1978

This T-shirt has a nature-themed background that emphasizes Dylan's reputation as an American troubadour. It is interesting that he holds an electric guitar against the pastoral landscape, while the back of the shirt features Dylan playing acoustic.

Bob Dylan *1978*

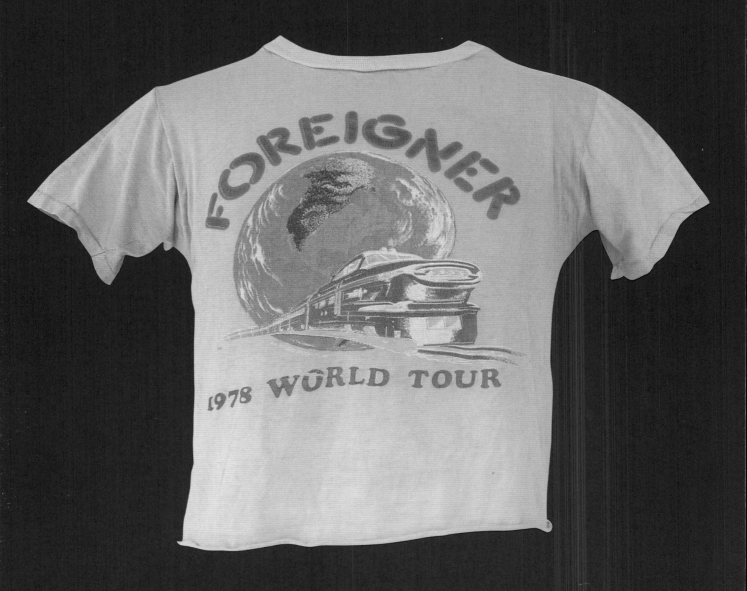

Pastel colors are unique to rock tees from the late '70s and early '80s, however, a travel theme was not uncommon.

Foreigner 1978

This amazing T-shirt does an excellent job of conveying the intensity of classic Black Sabbath. Since many heavy metal artists would credit Black Sabbath as a key influence, it is interesting to note that this is one of the earliest shirts to incorporate themes of violence and war—two major motifs of '80s metal tees.

Black Sabbath *1978*

Though the bold four-color spectrum and thick lines are consistent throughout this group of bootleg shirts, each tee is quite specific to the artist it promotes. The tee for Jethro Tull showcases elements of fantasy, while the one for Jeff Beck has no secondary imagery—consistent with Beck's understated look and classic rock sound. The Yes shirt is a low-budget approximation of the group's intricate album artwork, reflective of their nuanced sound.

Clockwise:
Jethro Tull *1978* **(front and back)**
Jeff Beck *ca. 1978*
Yes *1978*

A perfect example of why, contrary to some opinions, bootleg T-shirts are not inferior to licensed merchandise. This Who shirt "pops" due to strong design and bold use of color. It also has possibly the coolest representation of a guitar player with its midair depiction of Pete Townshend. The back of the shirt is a tribute to the group's recently deceased drummer, Keith Moon.

The Who *ca. 1978*

Proof that technical wizardry will never trump good design, this Sex Pistols T-shirt (above) features a classic image immediately recognizable to any Pistols fan, while the Iggy shirt (below) is a nod to the singer's playful aspect with the less-than-menacing purple ink on a cream background. Both shirts are, incidentally, distinctly of their era in style; the Sex Pistols shirt is banded at the collar and sleeves, and the Iggy Pop shirt is pastel. Neither of these T-shirt styles was popular after the very early '80s.

Sex Pistols *ca. 1978*
Iggy Pop *1978*

The print on this bootleg Rolling Stones T-shirt was used for several tours. The image has been seen on tees commemorating both the 1978 and 1981 Stones concert runs. This particular shirt is undated, though still marked as a tour shirt. It's all just further proof that savvy bootleggers were always looking to maximize profits.

The Rolling Stones *ca. 1978*

Boston *ca. 1979*

Frequently, bootleggers would take graphics from licensed merchandise or album covers, or even just classic images of the artist, and slap a simplistic reproduction on "unofficial" T-shirts; fans recognized the images despite the crude printing. Much of the appeal of vintage bootleg tees today is this evidence of human error—something that cannot be duplicated or approximated. That said, even licensed shirts sometimes utilized basic band art from other promotional materials for a cool tee design.

Scorpions *1979*
Bruce Springsteen *ca. 1979*

FRAMPTON COMES ALIVE

This Peter Frampton T-shirt is early proof of the increasing importance of the "guitar god" concept in rock-and-roll folklore. Compare it to older tees featured in this book for other guitar icons, such as Jimi Hendrix and Jeff Beck. Only now is the guitar shown front and center.

Two shirts from Alice Cooper's Madhouse Rock tour, both of which play up Alice's campy, ghoulish persona. One (above) relies on illustrations of spiders and goblins (also utilizing gold glitter—still visible across the top—to accentuate the fun, theatrical vibe) while the other (below) uses a font styled like dripping blood.

Alice Cooper *1979*
Alice Cooper *1979*

Economic creativity in action! This highly unusual Led Zeppelin tee features a graphic touting their 1977 U.S. tour on the front—and a design for the 1979 tour on the back! Is this T-shirt hard proof of the bottom line influencing rock T-shirt design (the recycling of an unsold shirt) or just a novel approach to creating a unique product to entice notoriously rabid Led Zeppelin fans?

Led Zeppelin *1979*

This quaint dinosaur graphic would reappear on future Monsters of Rock Festival tees (the concert was an annual event) with various icons and logos added depending on who was performing. This was one of the first recurrent festival T-shirts to have a branded look.

Monsters of Rock Festival *1979*

A beautiful shirt which utilizes the live performance montage screen print which was so popular on rock tees in the late '70s and early '80s.

Jethro Tull *ca. 1979*

By the end of the decade, even bands that only enjoyed cult popularity could afford to print up T-shirts; cheap to make, easy to move, and simple to sell, they were guaranteed moneymakers. Low-cost, single-color print jobs could still make cool shirts, like this one for Dixie Dregs.

Dixie Dregs *ca. 1979*

This bootleg KISS T-shirt is not very sophisticated, but, at the time, neither was the band. The comic-like graphics, primary colors, and glitter perfectly capture the over-the-top theatricality that has made KISS rock-and-roll legends. Incidentally, the glitter ink on this tee was a briefly popular novelty that only appeared on rock shirts in the late '70s.

KISS *ca. 1979*

Shirts with banded collars and sleeves were used only briefly by the rock T-shirt industry during the late '70s and very early '80s.
It is likely that, subconsciously, for fans, the more tailored look of these shirts seemed incongruent with rock and roll.

Queen *ca. 1979*
The Cars *ca. 1979*

A bootleg holiday tee, this shirt (above left) is quintessential Frank Zappa—it manages to be vulgar, humorous, quaint, and bizarre all at once. The performance collage imagery on shirts like this one for Fleetwood Mac (above right) spoke to the tremendous importance and excitement of seeing a favorite band in concert. Going to a show was a major social event.

Frank Zappa ca. *1979*
Fleetwood Mac *1979*

Richard Hell

Photo: Roberta Bayley

The author of seminal punk anthem "Blank Generation" and central member of classic punk bands the Heartbreakers, Television, and the Voidoids, Richard Hell was a precocious poet who arrived in New York City's lower east side in the late '60s by way of Lexington, Kentucky. A born innovator, his sound and look were critical influences in the burgeoning punk movement of the '70s. Indeed, Hell is often credited as the pioneer of the punk aesthetic: A wiry body; choppy hair; fitted, worn-out clothes; and, of course, a ripped and written-on self-styled T-shirt.

In fact, Hell was among the first of the outsider artists to recognize the potential of the T-shirt as a medium of communication and creative expression. As he states, "Something that appealed to me about rock and roll from the first was the way that bands communicated things in so many different ways, whether or not they even knew it. Take hairdos for instance—hair is just as important as anything a musician says in words. Elvis was very polite in everything he said in public, but his hair wasn't." Naturally, wardrobe could, and did, have the same impact.

It was this insight into the influence of rock music and its performers that encouraged Hell to explore his own style. "Writing and drawing on T-shirts was one idea I had of a way to say things, as was wearing them with holes in them," he says. The look rejected the fitted, colorful tees that were so popular with mainstream America, and it was radically different from the silkscreened T-shirts that were made to promote major recording artists in the mid '70s—but then so was the music. According to punk sensibility, money and skill didn't trump action and sincerity. Hell's T-shirt stylings reflected that grassroots earnestness. As he notes, "Just as important as any message that might be written in words, though, was the built-in message of those styles—that anybody could do it; you didn't have to buy what companies tried to tell you was good-looking, and you didn't have to have any money."

Hell's T-shirts were plain, decorated with simple geometric designs, ironic phrases, or band names. The words or graphics were scrawled on the fabric, usually in ink—seemingly just before the shirt was worn—resulting in a compellingly raw and immediate appearance. "Part of the point of the shirts I made was that you did them yourself," Hell explains. "All the shirts I made were 'editions of one' like that." His tees were never silkscreened or designed for sale. And though he wore most of his designs himself, Hell never donned his most infamous: a simple T-shirt with "Please Kill Me" stenciled across the front (he convinced a bandmate to wear it instead). That T-shirt alone has become something of a music-industry legend, with various rumors and stories circulated about its exact design and origin; the iconic phrase was even adopted as the title of the definitive book on New York punk. What's more, svengali Malcolm McLaren saw Richard Hell in New York and was so impressed with his style that he returned to England and used Hell as his guiding inspiration in creating the ratty look of punk legends the Sex Pistols.

But as sure as Richard Hell revolutionized fashion—and rock tees—he hasn't made a fortune off of the innovation. Precisely because the look was renegade do-it-yourself, it couldn't be copied and sold for profit (and it should be noted that profit was never Hell's driving goal with his art or ingenuity). That said, Hell easily admits, "I'm not against silkscreens on principle or anything, though." Today, more than twenty years after leaving music to pursue writing full-time, T-shirts emblazoned with "Richard Hell," "Television," and "Blank Generation" are sold internationally. Some are available through Hell's Web site (www.richardhell.com), and many more can be found in boutiques across the country and as far away as Japan. Though the shirts don't resemble any of Hell's classic, handmade icons, many do incorporate vintage graphics. "Musicians (and writers) at my level of celebrity don't make much of a living from their work directly. Not as much as a decent insurance salesman," states Hell. "If someone's going to be making money from my name or picture or work, it ought to be me."

Metal Health: Rocl

Throughout the '80s the rock T-shirt industry continued to evolve. Notably, the second decade of rock T-shirts saw a greater effort on the part of artists, record labels, and related companies to control the phenomenon. Corresponding with the crackdown on bootlegging, the industry expanded its retail strategies, which resulted in the growth of sales. With more official product being released and benefiting from the marketing and design savvy of large merchandising companies, '80s rock tees have a decidedly more polished look than their '70s counterparts. Indeed, superior printing capabilities and increased industry professionalism resulted in an array of bold designs during the mid-decade zenith of rock T-shirts. The most ubiquitous of subculture status symbols, rock T-shirts in the '80s were big business.

Once it was clear that rock T-shirts were a major moneymaker, everyone involved wanted to protect their investments. Winterland Productions had introduced the increasingly costly practice of licensing artists by the late '70s, so companies that planned to stay in business were forced to expand not only their design and printing capabilities, but also their retail opportunities. According to industry veteran Paul Kallish, early in the decade, Great Southern Co., a merchandise company that handled many of the '80s top heavy metal acts, pioneered the selling of rock tees at established retail outlets like chain record stores. Wider market opportunities like this brought in more money, but also required that rock T-shirt manufacturers produced a greater number of designs for each artist. Meanwhile, though parking lot bootleggers still flourished, a serious effort to curtail unlicensed merchandise had begun, led in part by the '80s first supergroup, Van Halen (check out lead singer David Lee Roth's autobiography, *Crazy from the Heat,* for extended details on the harrowing experience, including a hotel sit-down with a bootleg T-shirt kingpin).

Reflecting the general fashions of the times, in the early '80s sleeveless rock T-shirts were a trend, as were—briefly—sleeveless sweatshirts. Baseball jerseys with three-quarter-length sleeves in a color contrasting to the shirt's body were also favorites. The '80s are similarly notable for widespread use of 50-50 cotton-polyester blend T-shirts. These tees had the advantages of being cheap, light, and able to hold ink well through many washings (though it must be said that they also stimulated body odor due to the limited "breathability" of

Tees in the 1980s

the fabric). The thinness of the fabric made the T-shirts clingy, creating the iconic, slim rock tee silhouette which, intentionally or not, accentuated the music's overt sexuality. But by the late '80s, rock tees became larger (in sync with an overall fashion shift midway through the decade) and were more likely to be printed on bulkier mid-weight 100% cotton T-shirts, particularly if licensed merchandise.

Design-wise, rock tees in the early '80s continued many late-'70s trends, including multi-color print jobs and "busy" or cluttered graphics. Incorporating band members' images in the T-shirt design remained popular, though they were more likely to be depicted in a staged scene rather than mid-performance. And while punks had experimented with "personalizing" T-shirts via handwriting and cutting in the later part of the '70s, wider audiences didn't try customizing rock shirts until a few years later—sometimes cropping the tees and cutting off or slashing the sleeves. (The Girlschool and Mötley Crüe *Theatre of Pain* shirts in this section are good examples of this trend.)

Curiously, during the Regan era, certain bands also had mascots which began to appear on their T-shirts, often as stand-ins for the band members themselves. Most notably, this is true for Iron Maiden, whose corpse-like figure, Eddie, appeared on the majority of their shirts and with Allister Fiend, the depraved-rocker character who popped up on many Mötley Crüe tees from *Shout at the Devil* (1983) through *Girls, Girls, Girls* (1987).

Throughout the decade, the dominant trends in rock T-shirt graphics were cartoon illustrations and images of bands in overly dramatic scenes, as well as various monster motifs. Lighter rock and hair-metal bands tended toward the cartoonish designs, while heavier bands aimed to assert their intensity through more evil or apocalyptic art. Death, dying, violence, and flirtatious touches of Satanism are all themes typical to '80s tees. Sexualized images of fantasy women—heavy metal interpretations of pin-up art—also appear. Almost across the board, '80s rock tees made a concerted effort to suggest or depict antisocial tendencies. Perhaps the need to reiterate rock's badass stereotype was particularly important due to the increasing commercialization and mainstream acceptance of the music genre (thanks, in no small part, to MTV).

This Lynyrd Skynyrd shirt showcases a design far more detailed than tees from just five or so years previous. Improved printing techniques also allowed for a more subtle use of color.

Lynyrd Skynyrd *1980*

Pat Travers might never have been a major rock star, but this shirt leaves no doubt as to what he was about. It is straightforward rock-and-roll imagery at its best: in-your-face energy and intensity.

Pat Travers *1980*

Though this Ted Nugent shirt simply repeats well-known album art, there is nonetheless something very intimate about putting the image of a man wearing a loincloth on your chest—it speaks to the incredible devotion of rock fans.

Ted Nugent *1980*

Both of these shirts were made for Queen's *The Game* tour—one is licensed (above) and one is bootleg (below).
Though the official tee clearly benefits from superior printing and a complex design, it is hard not to be drawn
in by the bootleg's flashy appeal and front-and-center use of the band's image.

Queen *1980*
Queen *1980*

The simple rendering of this recognizable Bruce Springsteen album image is as direct as the Boss's sound and presentation.

Bruce Springsteen ca. *1980*

While bootleg shirts often have less sophisticated prints, part of the reason they remain so popular is because they almost always acknowledge one of fans' most cherished elements of rock and roll: the rock stars themselves. The images on these tees may be crude, but they also show that the idols themselves, even more than the actual concert, are the main attraction.

REO Speedwagon *1980*
RUSH *1980*

Bootleg Van Halen tees, like this one is, are quite rare due to the band's crusade against unlicensed merchandise. In fact, the persistent efforts of Van Halen, Journey, and Billy Joel at the start of the '80s were a major factor in the decline of unlicensed merchandise, for all artists, throughout the decade. This T-shirt is also notable because, design-wise, it is caught between two decades: The back image shows Van Halen in full-tilt performance—the montage motif popular during the '70s—but also has flames coming out of Alex Van Halen's drumsticks—a touch of the more symbolic T-shirt imagery which became standard in the '80s.

Van Halen *1980*

A competitive market and the increased availability of quality printing systems made four- and six-color designs de rigueur by the early '80s. The increased use of color made '80s rock tees stand out; it also allowed for more complex designs. All of these tees are from this era, but their images are reflective of popular '70s rock-tee design, aligning the artists with a classic rock sound through the straightforward, centered graphics.

.38 Special *ca. 1981*
The Allman Brothers Band *1981*
April Wine *1981*

Compared to Black Sabbath's intense '70s imagery, this tee makes it clear that the group was heading in a new direction. Numerous '80s heavy metal stars cited Sabbath as inspiration, so it is interesting that the demonic and satanic imagery on this shirt was iconography that became increasingly popular throughout the decade, symbolic of heavy metal's dangerous and deviant reputation.

Black Sabbath *1981*

Certainly one of the most visually identifiable rock bands, the Grateful Dead have many wonderful T-shirt designs. This one is particularly engaging, as it incorporates the group's mascot skeletons with an easily recognizable San Francisco landscape and starry night sky to represent the band's home base and signature dreamy sound.

Grateful Dead *1981*

This vibrant bootleg T-shirt lands Journey's well-known scarab icon in a rush of energy. The design can be seen as symbolic of either Journey's soaring sound or surging popularity. Interestingly, the tiny stars forming a border for this T-shirt's main graphic also pop up on a number of bootleg rock shirts from the same year (for instance, some Rolling Stones and Pat Benatar shirts featured in this book). Perhaps all of the shirts are the work of the same artist?

Journey *1981*

Baseball jerseys were a popular rock tee style from the early to mid '80s. This one made for Judas Priest sports an impressively off-center screen print, unusual even for a bootleg.

Judas Priest *1981*

Grateful Dead merchandise has one of the most consistent looks in rock and roll because the same artists (Stanley Mouse and Alton Kelley) worked with the band for years. Consequently, Grateful Dead shirts look specific to the Grateful Dead, rather than the era. But because of the band's widespread popularity and influence, as well as their lengthy career, the Grateful Dead aesthetic—namely, skulls and flowers—is a cornerstone of rock iconography.

Grateful Dead *1981*

Ozzy Osbourne *1981*

This incredible Ozzy Osbourne shirt from Canada commemorates his first solo tour. The KKK imagery is extremely strange—
Ozzy has never been affiliated with the group or espoused their beliefs—so it seems most likely that the design of this T-shirt
is the result of a bootlegger's misguided attempt to inventively illustrate the Diary of a Madman tour.

The Rolling Stones *1981*

Though they had already been around for nearly twenty years, the Rolling Stones were still hot when they toured in 1981. These shirts illustrate the increasing difference between licensed and bootleg T-shirts by the early '80s. The official tour shirt (opposite page), features a great twist on the band's iconic tongue logo. By contrast, the shirt above is a bootleg that, while quite captivating, does not have the design sophistication or band specificity that has made the other tee, the vintage Stones shirt, most coveted by fans. The tongue logo shirt is readable from a distance—the graphic is relatively simple—the black shirt makes for a perfect rock tee. The combination of the two makes for a classic promotion of the Stones' roots rock and roll. By contrast, the image on this bootleg tour tee is only recognizable as the Rolling Stones when viewed at close proximity, and the slightly stiff illustrated figures fail to convey the showmanship and energy that have made the Stones a legendary live act.

The Rolling Stones *1981*

Though the amateurish illustrations and sloppy print jobs of '80s bootleg tees are easily distinguished from the detailed six-color printing of their licensed counterparts, they nonetheless have an awkward charm that is quite unique. Bootleg tees also tend to have great immediate impact, because their graphics are less nuanced and, thus, easier to take in.

Clockwise:
Rainbow *1981*
Judas Priest *1981*
Triumph *1981*
Pat Benatar *1981*

This shirt features detailed album art, yet seems to be a bootleg because the color palette is that special mix of bright basics—red, yellow, blue—that is consistent among professional bootlegs.

Rush *1981*

Van Halen first hit it big with their debut album in 1978, and this tee shows their '70s roots with the performance montage design. However, the design is greatly enhanced and modernized by the high-quality, cutting-edge photo graphics of each band member.

Van Halen *1981*

Like the official Rolling Stones 1981 tour tee used the American flag, this Kinks shirt incorporates the Union Jack into its design to distinguish the band as special, and especially cool. After the rush of the British Invasion, and the stream of heavy rock and glam bands from England in the '70s, the early '80s saw a decline in English rock bands (the rockers went new wave!) so being English was significant. Note an illegible autograph on the shirt's left shoulder.

The Kinks *1981*

In the '80s, rock T-shirts did not always aim for a strict representation of a given band; performance illustrations and specific symbolism were sometimes replaced with imagery reflecting general rock-and-roll ideals—power, rebellion, deviance. These four shirts all sport graphics that suggest the music can't be contained or controlled: Aerosmith (top left), busts through the ceiling of a stadium, Van Halen (top right), rips through the front of the T-shirt, and, in a riff on their album cover, Scorpions (bottom right), shatter glass. The concept was even incorporated in bootleg shirts, like this one for Rainbow (bottom left).

Clockwise:
Aerosmith *1982*
Van Halen *1982*
Scorpions *1982*
Rainbow *1982*

This Uriah Heep jersey is another great example of the comic-book-inspired demon images which are key motifs of many '80s rock shirts. By the end of the decade, though, computers would render such fantastical hand-drawn illustrations of evil obsolete.

Uriah Heep *1982*

Two different takes on guitar god imagery. The focus and intensity is conveyed in both, and only font and wardrobe distinguish the pedigree.

Aldo Nova *1982*
Jimi Hendrix *1982*

The shadowed faces on these two shirts is not exemplary of a larger theme in rock T-shirt design—it is isolated to just a few early-'80s tees—but it perfectly captures an aura of danger and mystery that is part of rock's appeal.

Elvis Costello and the Attractions *1982*
Queen *1982*

One more terrific example of the diversity among T-shirts made for the same tour: One (above) uses a piercing portrait of Bowie for maximum debonair impact, while one (below) uses graphic illustration.

David Bowie *1982*
David Bowie *1982*

Led Zeppelin's magical, mystical vibe is tapped to the fullest effect by the myriad iconography in this better-quality bootleg. Made after the band's 1980 breakup, this shirt was likely sold in small, independent record stores or head shops with a special appeal for fans of classic rock and Dungeons and Dragons who also worshipped Led Zeppelin.

Led Zeppelin *1982*

While the graphics on '80s bootleg tees remained clunky, they were nonetheless more detailed than many of their counterparts from the previous decade. Background graphics and depth perspective were among the design improvements.

Clockwise:
Asia *1982*
The Who *1982*
Summer Jam Festival *1982*

These two different takes on Pat Benatar's *Get Nervous* album art highlight the effect print quality and professional designers have on T-shirt images.

Pat Benatar *1982*
Pat Benatar *1982*

The common rock iconography of flames is put to great use on this Sammy Hagar tee. Guitar gods were well established by the (Jimmy Page, Pete Townshend), and T-shirts from the decade often showed them mid-performance. Thus, '80s stars had to one-up in imagery. The tilted perspective and bold colors on this shirt do an excellent job of making relative newcomer Hagar larger tha

This simple tee for socially conscious punks the Clash might be considered an updated version of Richard Hell's iconic '70s "Please Kill Me" T-shirt. It reflects the group's aggressive politics.

The Clash *ca. 1982*

Clockwise:
Stray Cats *1982*
(front and back)
Pink Floyd *1982*
Journey *1982*
Survivor *1982*

By the early '80s, rock T-shirts were part of the standard wardrobe donned by many rock fans. Consequently, artists did not need to be represented on a T-shirt for it to recognizably be related to the music, so long as it followed the established tenets of rock-tee design: stylized band name across the chest, colorful graphic centered below. For instance, even if one wasn't familiar with the album cover art, it was easy to spot that Pink Floyd (opposite page) or Def Leppard (above) were bands, not sports teams or auto repair shops.

Clockwise:
Def Leppard *1983*
Iron Maiden *1983*
Rush *1983*
Oregon Jam *1983*
Blue Öyster Cult *1983*

Another novel approach to the celebration of guitar rock, this tee takes its cue from the *Flick of the Switch* album title to illustrate that AC/DC is supercharged.

AC/DC 1983

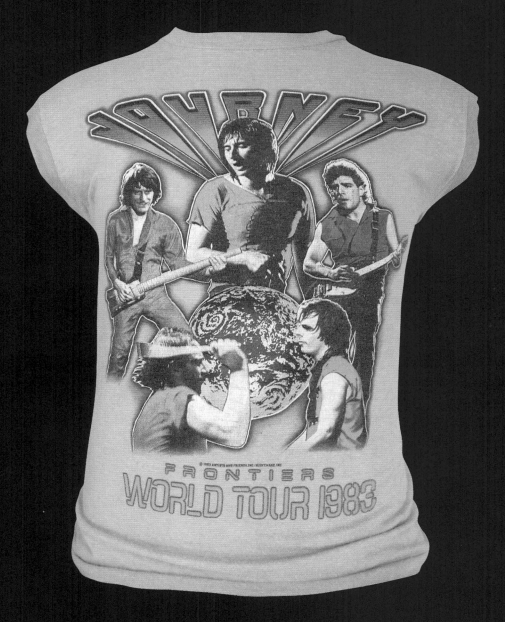

A subtle reflection of Journey's decade-straddling career, this 1983 tour shirt features a performance collage layout and benefits from the high-quality printing that was becoming standard in the '80s. Though popular since the late '70s, by mid-decade the performance collage layout would be out of fashion, as a new generation of musicians sought to redefine rock and roll and rock stardom.

Journey *1983*

These shirts exemplify two different approaches to representing a band as a gang, while also emphasizing how T-shirts were used to identify a group's sound and image as unique. The Judas Priest tee (above) incorporates some guitar god imagery with a band picture that captures Priest's tough leather-and-motorcycles heavy metal aesthetic. Meanwhile, the Molly Hatchet shirt (below) places the band within an Old West setting to reflect the group's countrified classic rock roots.

Judas Priest *ca. 1983*
Molly Hatchet *1983*

The Misfits were a major early-'80s punk band, and this T-shirt depicting skeletons in a dramatic setting has more in common iconographically with the '80s metal scene than first-wave punks. The skeletons with rad hair were consistent throughout Misfits artwork; it was a deft way of showing the band's dark mood had a sly edge.

Misfits *ca. 1983*

An early Mötley Crüe shirt, this tee is from their breakthrough *Shout at the Devil* period. Notice that this T-shirt doesn't feature a picture of the band performing, but instead shows them heavily costumed in a theatrical setting—a new look for a new decade.

Unlike the early-'70s tees which showcased simple portraits of rock stars on sunny-colored T-shirts (cream, yellow, sky blue), the faces of '80s idols were slapped on black T-shirts, as black became the definitive color of rock and roll.

Billy Idol *1983*

This tee is a weird mishmash of recognizable Pink Floyd artwork, designed to reflect the band's lengthy career.

Pink Floyd *ca. 1983*

Another great Sammy Hagar shirt, this tee ingeniously manages to be sexy
without being crass or explicit like many of the decade's rock T-shirts.

Sammy Hagar *1983*

The divergent designs of two Neil Young shirts from the same concert tour were likely offered to tap into differing sensibilities within Young's broad fan base. The shirt above presents him as a mythic, larger-than-life figure, while the other (below) shows a relatable troubador.

Neil Young *1983*
Neil Young *1983*

Among the first metal acts to hit it big, Quiet Riot helped establish heavy metal imagery. Insanity and representations of asylums and restraints, along with demons and satanism, were popular throughout the decade.

Quiet Riot *ca. 1983*

Even though these bootleg tees lifted their images directly off of album covers, the graphics take on a new, raw feel by being reduced to a primary color palette.

ZZ Top *1983*

The giant head of Dee Snider (Twisted Sister's singer) on this shirt perfectly captures the group's in-your-face look and sound.

Twisted Sister *1983*

Not looking as though they were adapted from live concert photos, the graphics on these shirts use action images as an innovative way to capture the energy of rock and roll.

Bruce Springsteen *1984*
Joan Jett and the Blackhearts *1984*

The demonic and dark imagery on rock shirts like these was central to the perception of heavy metal as tough and menacing.

Clockwise:
W.A.S.P. *1984*
(front and back)
Dio *1984*

Though punks began experimenting with customizing their clothes in the '70s, cutting T-shirts didn't catch on with more mainstream rock audiences until the early '80s.

Iron Maiden *1984*
Girlschool *1984*

According to an industry insider, a similar middle finger design was intended for an early-'70s Badfinger tee, but the shirt printer found the graphic offensive and so screened it sideways.

Great White *1984*

Props and scenery became increasingly important to rock tees through the '80s, as in this Judas Priest shirt which doesn't feature the group's lead singer singing but, rather, astride a fierce motorcycle.

Judas Priest *1984*

As printing standards and technology improved, rock T-shirts flaunted more detailed, photo-realistic images of bands rather than interpretive illustrations or primitive prints. The Cars shirt (bottom left) is a particularly interesting mix of high-quality illustration and photo-reproduction printing, with the band members' faces peeking through the windshield of a Duster.

Clockwise:
KISS *1984*
Scorpions *1984*
The Pretenders *1984*
The Cars *1984*

In the '80s, tees also began using images of sexy women to sell rock and roll.

Krokus *1984*
Nazareth *1984*

The pixelation of cheap screen printing is reminiscent of comic book art; it blurs the line between reality and fiction.
On this tee, it seems a perfect reflection of Jim Morrison's posthumous mythic-rock-god reputation.

The Doors *ca. 1984*

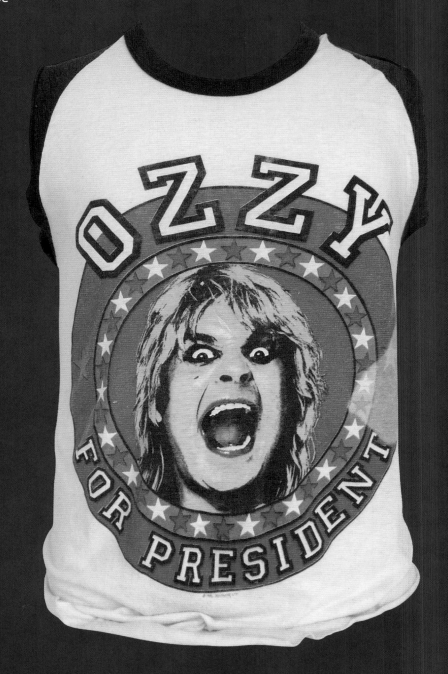

A very cool rock T-shirt from Texas, this shirt's slogan highlights fans' loyalty and commitment to their favorite artists.

Ozzy Osbourne *1984*

For a band whose name had no references to nature, Van Halen was particularly fond of incorporating the power and aggression of animals into their T-shirt designs. An earlier tee featured a lion; this shirt sports an eagle.

Van Halen *1984*

A central graphic which reflected the band's name, album, or a song title—instead of a specifically rock-and-roll—inspired graphic or group image—became common on '80s rock tees.

Clockwise:
Ratt *1984*
Zebra *1984*
Triumph *1984*

While it was acceptable to portray music artists just as they are (e.g., performers) on early rock shirts, throughout the '80s it was important to play them up as larger than life. Showing rock stars—for instance Blackie Lawless, lead singer of W.A.S.P. (above right)—as insane, aggressive, or wild were common portrayals. The Ratt tee (bottom left) is an interesting twist on the concept, as it shows a rabid rodent getting a sonic lobotomy on a soundboard.

Clockwise:
Twisted Sister *1984*
W.A.S.P. *1984*
Ratt *1984*

Cartoon graphics—as opposed to the '70s illustrations—were popular on '80s rock tees, particularly for punk and fringe artists. That said, the sentiments of the shirts fit within rock's overall pose: aggressive, disturbed, reckless, and socially menacing.

Circle Jerks *1985*
Corrosion of Conformity *ca. 1985*

This is possibly the only royal purple rock T-shirt ever made.
(It's worth noting that the only color never used for original rock tees is kelly green.)

Deep Purple *1985*

Bands in the '80s often had mascots which stood in for the group members themselves on T-shirts. The depraved-rocker character Allister Fiend appeared on many Mötley Crüe shirts produced between *Shout at the Devil* (1983) and *Girls, Girls, Girls* (1987), proudly representing the band's wild reputation and high-adrenaline music. Incidentally, this tee is perhaps the only of its kind in the rock T-shirt pantheon: The backside of the shirt sports a public service announcement "Don't drink and drive." This is unusual for any rock band, but doubly so for the notoriously hard-partying, substance-abusing Crüe. (The band's lead singer, Vince Neil, was convicted of drunk driving following a deadly car accident in 1984, which is likely the reason for the incongruity of a PSA on a rock shirt.)

Mötley Crüe *1985*

Heavier metal bands were particularly devoted to tees depicting demons, death, war, and violence to promote their darker sound.

Clockwise:
Dio *1985*
Iron Maiden *1985*
Slayer *ca. 1985*
Megadeth *ca. 1985*

Less flamboyant bands like Tom Petty and the Heartbreakers and Dire Straits didn't pander to guitar-god rock mythology (they aren't even pictured on their shirts), but their tees still reiterated that the guitar was *the* instrument central to rock and roll.

Dire Straits *1985*
Tom Petty and the Heartbreakers *1985*

Who knew Billy Idol was black? The low-quality standards for bootleg tees allowed for some strange graphics.

Billy Idol *ca. 1986*

'80s punk had a strong fan base, but it was still only a minor commercial success compared to heavy metal. Consequently, punk tees from the decade did not benefit from major funding—they tend to be simpler and less colorful (and thus, less costly to produce) than their more mainstream rock T-shirt counterparts. But they are nonetheless very cool, and often have an intentionally humorous edge.

Dead Kennedys *ca. 1986*
GBH *1986*

This is a rare T-shirt for Seattle rock legends Green River—widely considered one of the star pioneers of the grunge sound. (Members of the group went on to form Mudhoney, Mother Love Bone, and Pearl Jam.) Though the band members all sport the long hair and lean bodies key for '80s rock success, they don't have the glammed-out wardrobes or theatrical attitudes of their contemporaries, the heavy metal stars. It is a subtle indication that the direction of rock music in the northwest was changing from the national norm.

Green River *ca. 1986*

Tie-dyeing was quite uncommon among rock T-shirts, particularly for the heavier bands, so this
Iron Maiden tee is something of an anomaly. The image of a tweaked corpse with guns ablaze communicates
the darkness of the band and somehow makes the peace-and-love tie-dye seem kind of tough.

Iron Maiden *ca. 1986*

The graphic on this Bon Jovi shirt (above left) seems out of sync with the band's arena pop-rock image. Indeed, the skull, captain's hat, and aviator sunglasses are more the streetwise style of Guns N' Roses. This rock tee of Jake E. Lee (above right) deviates slightly from the standard rock shirt design format: The artist's name does not appear across the chest and above the image.

Bon Jovi *ca. 1986*
Jake E. Lee *ca. 1986*

Here are two versions of the Ramones logo tee, which is possibly the most iconic rock T-shirt. Arturo Vega, the group's creative director and designer of the logo, conceived it to contrast any impression of the group as cartoonish. The white shirt (above) is an official tour shirt, while the orange (below) is likely a bootleg print as it is missing a few of the key design intricacies of the Ramones seal. The white one lists the band members as Joey, Johnny, Dee Dee, and Richie; Richie was not the original drummer (that would be Tommy Ramone, whose name is on the bootleg), but he played with the band for much of the '80s. Most reproduction T-shirts sold today feature the original Ramones seal, with the names Joey, Johnny, Dee Dee, and Tommy.

The Ramones *1986*
The Ramones *ca. 1986*

Even as the use of six or more colors in printing became more available and popular throughout the decade, bootleg tees usually stuck to four colors (to keep the cost down). Bootlegs were also more likely to have basic, uncomplicated graphics. As a result, there is a clear difference between the look of licensed and unofficial T-shirts in the '80s. This Jim Morrison tee may be unlicensed, but it still looks great.

Jim Morrison ca. 1986

These are two different shirts for L.A. Guns' first tour, Sex, Booze, and Tattoos. The shirt above is particularly evocative—the artwork combining elements of the group's guns-and-badge logo with illustrations of sleazy women is pure Sunset Strip "cock rock." (This is the glitter-influenced, hook-laden metal and pop rock phenomenon that dominated '80s MTV. The music was rarely political, usually sexual, and frequently dismissed as totally vapid. Bands of this genre were quite stylized in appearance, often done up to near drag-queen levels, but very macho in attitude. L.A. Guns added a vampiric element to this mix.) The ubiquituous '80s rock tee icon, the skull, is thrown in, too, for good measure.

L.A. Guns *1988*
L.A. Guns *1988*

Stryper was a Christian metal band, but you would never know it unless you read the fine print on their T-shirt.

Stryper ca. 1986

Slayer shirts are among the most popular vintage rock tees today. Somehow, the band's tees managed to have the best skulls, demons, and monsters, which were among the most popular '80s motifs.

Slayer ca. *1986*

This tee puts a glitzy, exotic twist on wet T-shirt contest imagery, but the sunglasses are what make it totally ZZ Top. (That Ray-Ban look is totally '80s, too.)

ZZ Top 1986

By the mid-to-late-'80s, screen-printing techniques were greatly improving. The graphics on rock tees became increasingly complicated; the images more photo-realistic. The cartoon and illustrated graphics which define the aesthetics of earlier rock tees increasingly gave way to computer-generated images. Bands like Bon Jovi and Poison had many fans that were attracted by the big hair and pretty faces of the groups' members, so it was important to put them front and center on the shirts. In fact, big '80s hair could make just about any T-shirt rock.

Clockwise:
Bon Jovi *1986*
Poison *1986*
TNT *ca. 1987*
Def Leppard *1987*

In keeping with the harder edge of '80s rock, this Alice Cooper tee doesn't have the camp quality
that defined his '70s shirts, though it definitely has not dropped his macabre aesthetics.

Alice Cooper *1987*

Cartoon graphics and a stylized heavy metal guitar make this Great White T-shirt (above left) an
'80s rock-tee time capsule. Though it simply features the cover art for *Appetite for Destruction*,
this Guns N' Roses tee (above right) is still among the most recognizable, popular rock T-shirts.

Great White *ca. 1987*
Guns N' Roses *1987*

This Megadeth T-shirt isn't thematically different from earlier heavy metal T-shirts, but the graphic is much more detailed. The charcoal color of the shirt is the result of black fading due to countless washings. Today, reproduction rock tees are sometimes printed on shirts dyed this color to create a vintage rock look.

Megadeth *1987*

Metal Up Your Ass was the original title of the Metallica album which came to be called *Kill 'Em All*.
This shirt was printed with glow-in-the-dark ink—a cool new innovation at the time.

Metallica *1987*

These two Whitesnake shirts are both licensed merchandise from the same year, so comparing them offers a great peak at the changes occurring within the look of rock T-shirts by the later '80s. The black tee (above) features lead singer David Coverdale performing—it is a high-resolution image like those that would be standard by the end of the decade and into the '90s. The jersey (below) on the other hand, has the classic '80s rock T-shirt aesthetic—a centered, framed graphic without any sense of technical wizardry to the design.

Whitesnake *1987*
Whitesnake *1987*

The graphics on this Megadeth shirt distance it from the band's earlier tees. Though the image is classic Megadeth, with the apocalyptic iconography popular to '80s metal, the slick technology necessary to print at this quality makes the T-shirt feel mass-produced.

Megadeth *1987*

Exodus 1988

The impaled skull: definitive heavy metal iconography of the '80s.

Metallica *1988*
Metallica *1988*

By the late '80s, the look of rock tees was rapidly changing, thanks to the influence of computer-generated graphics and new printing technologies. The sizing of the shirts was skewing larger, and typography was becoming larger, too. Rather than featuring a central, framed image, rock shirts increasingly had big block print. Guitarist Angus Young is AC/DC's mascot on this tee, like many before. But this tour shirt has brighter colors and more nuanced printing than earlier tour tees. Likewise, the graphic takes up more space on the shirt.

AC/DC *1988*

Photo-realistic printing brings KISS to life in a whole new way on this Crazy Nights tour shirt.

KISS *1988*

Dirty Rotten Imbeciles *1988*

This Dirty Rotten Imbeciles T-shirt (opposite) has a grassroots, low-budget appeal which testifies to the punk-
metal band's cult following. The colors on this Ozzy Osbourne tee (above) are extremely bright—something
that wasn't possible at the start of his solo career (1980). In all other respects, the graphics on this shirt would
not be out of place in the early '80s. Illustrations of a fleeing crowd were popular on mid-'80s metal shirts.

Ozzy Osbourne *1988*

The layout of this shirt is much like that of earlier Slayer tees—a large face across the chest with no additional imagery—but, technically, the print is much more sophisticated. By maintaining the classic Slayer style, the shirt doesn't lose its intimacy to the high-tech printing (which was the case with many other artists).

Slayer ca. *1988*

Queensrÿche was just getting started with their recording career in the late '80s; consequently, it is not surprising that this early T-shirt for the band bears none of the trappings of classic '80s rock tees. With the big, unadorned promo picture of the band across the front, this shirt previews the direction rock shirt design would take in the '90s—a much less playful medium.

Queensrÿche *1988*

The photo-realistic human images on these tees give them a new, mass-produced feel, even though they probably were not manufactured in any greater quantity than rock tees throughout the decade.

Faster Pussycat *1989*
Billy Squier *ca. 1989*

The illustrated graphics on these two tees are totally '80s—high-voltage mayhem—with seemingly no awareness of the changing climate in rock T-shirt design at the end of the decade.

Exodus *1989*
Kix *1989*

The bright colors and photo-realistic print on this tee reflect the changing look of rock T-shirt design, but the pose is classic metal; in fact, this image for King Diamond seems to be a direct descendant of early-'80s W.A.S.P.

King Diamond *1989*

Jane's Addiction *1989*

These two Jane's Addiction tees show the evolving direction of rock T-shirts at the close of the '80s. The shirts are more generously cut, and the graphics cover the entire front of the shirt. Similarly, neither shirt features any of the standard '80s rock symbolism, but instead both are printed with pared-down, clean images. A new band setting a new tone for a new decade.

Jane's Addiction *1989*

Though this Mötley Crüe shirt is from the end of the decade, it still bears imagery typical to '80s metal—a sword, a demon, and bimbos—which is only fitting, as Mötley Crüe pioneered the genre.

Mötley Crüe *1989*

By the late '80s, most new metal bands were bypassing original artwork for their T-shirts and instead just printing high-resolution copies of album covers or band photos (above) shown large across the front of the tee.

Skid Row *ca. 1989*

Arturo Vega

You don't have to love the Ramones to know the Ramones—their iconic T-shirts are everywhere.

For that you can thank their long-time creative director and friend, Arturo Vega.

Originally from Chihuahua, Mexico, Arturo was an artist living in New York City's lower east side when he met Douglas Colvin (soon to become Dee Dee Ramone) in 1973. Dee Dee liked Arturo's painting style and wanted him to become involved with the band he was forming. In 1974, Arturo began working with the Ramones, helping them set up for gigs and designing their first *Village Voice* ads. Though he teamed up with the fledgling band for what he thought would be merely a digression from painting, those years turned into decades, and the Ramones turned into legends. Attending all but two of the Ramones 2,263 live concerts, Arturo was with them all along, helping craft the band's image and overseeing all of their visuals—from poster design to album cover art, stage backdrops to concert lighting—for more than two decades.

Just as significant, he's the man behind the group's beloved T-shirts, too.

When the Ramones got going in 1974, rock shirts were still a relatively new phenomenon. They were a product reserved for major recording artists and rock icons; this radical band from Queens was anything but. Though T-shirts of all varieties comprised a key element of the Ramones' uniform (along with black leather jackets, torn jeans, and flat-soled sneakers), self-promoting rock tees seemed far-fetched to the oddball band. Arturo made Ramones shirts for band members and their close associates, but no one in the group believed that anyone within the greater public would want to identify themselves—via T-shirts—with such a bunch of misfits. They didn't think Ramones shirts would sell.

Nonetheless, when the band's record label refused to pay for Arturo to go on tour in 1977, he was forced to find a creative way to cover his travel expenses while accompanying the group. Already working as the Ramones' lighting director, he decided to print up Ramones T-shirts and supervise their sale at concerts, too. These original tees featured the iconic Ramones logo (also designed by Arturo, with input from Tommy Ramone) silkscreened onto blank shirts purchased in Greenwich Village for $2.50 each.

This idea born of necessity proved to be a very fortuitous change. From 1977 to today,

Ramones T-shirts have been a profitable venture. Though the Ramones were never a commercial success, they have always been cult favorites with a devoted following and T-shirt sales were their most significant source of income. The Ramones wisely retained total control over their T-shirts for much of that time, and were more involved in their making than probably any other major band. During the late '70s and early '80s, band members would often return to Arturo's loft after shows at punk club CBGB (conveniently located around the corner) to silkscreen the shirts themselves—prompting neighbors to complain about the toxic smell emitted by the inks. On overseas tours, "each band member would take a trunk filled with T-shirts," Arturo recalls, ensuring the merchandise table didn't run out halfway through the tour. Arturo managed the operation throughout the life of the band, and he continues to oversee Ramones licensing to this day. From buying blank T-shirts, (originally this included a lot of youth sizes, worn by adults to achieve that perfect punk, tight fit) to supervising their printing, to conceiving the designs, he has been intimately involved with Ramones T-shirts for nearly thirty years. Currently, he is the creative force on the team of people who manage more than twenty licenses with companies producing Ramones merchandise internationally. His involvement with Ramones shirts is among the longest careers in the rock T-shirt industry, and probably the oldest ongoing merchandise relationship between an individual and a band.

"Today, the Ramones have sold more T-shirts than records, without a doubt," says Arturo. "Remember, they never had a major hit. Only one album went gold." But probably no other band has the same reputation for underground integrity, either. In today's mass-produced, chain-store world, the Ramones' commitment to their ideals—despite lack of mainstream acceptance—brands them as even more strikingly original. The Ramones are famous for underground authenticity almost as much as the sonic revolution they helped steer. Their T-shirts, consequently, are symbolic outside of the punk realm.

Arturo Vega is keenly aware that the Ramones' legacy has evolved. He is not terribly bothered by the fact that a portion of people sporting Ramones tees don't have a real knowledge or appreciation of the group's music. He recognizes that some folks purchase the tees as a means of buying into the Ramones credibility, because, "they never sold out," and he is proud of that aspect of the band's reputation. Whether they realize it or not, these casual consumers are supporting the band, keeping them in the public eye and encouraging new generations to wonder, "Just who are the Ramones?"

End of the Century:

If anything, rock T-shirts from the early '90s hint toward the impending backlash against rock and roll. The very things that made the new grunge and indie bands reject prototypical rock stardom were undermining the relevance of rock T-shirts, too. Continually increasing corporate involvement in the design of rock tees resulted in shirts that were staid instead of shocking, banal instead of cool. Computers allowed for even more colors and photo-realistic detail, but as these technological advancements were indulged, fashion and design concepts were increasingly overlooked. Bootleg shirts—which had often featured the most interesting, streetwise graphics—were becoming increasingly rare as a result of corporate vigilance. Making a rock shirt, like making a record, had become a bureaucratic enterprise that rarely resulted in a superior product.

As with all rock T-shirts, '90s tees mirrored the fashion sensibilities of their time. Embracing the trend started in the late '80s, '90s rock shirts were now made on thick 100 percent cotton oversized T-shirts. The popular way to wear these tees was unmodified and loose, creating a very low-key, slacker silhouette. The generous cut and drape of '90s tees reiterated the minimalist aesthetics of grunge and alternative rock, a sharp contrast to rock's previous paradigms.

Similarly, while the past two decades' rock shirts used various design motifs to play up a larger-than-life rock star sensibility, tees for '90s artists were decidedly understated. For instance, grunge bands did not indulge the concept of camera-ready rock stardom, so their shirts almost never featured just members of the band. Instead, rock's new notables chose to put a band logo or ironic image on their tees. Though concert shirts often continued to list tour stops, early-'90s shirts were just as likely to flaunt an insider phrase or term on the back. This approach emphasized the artists' ideological difference from '80s rock stardom: The generalized, cocky statements found on past rock tees (e.g., "We came, we saw, we kicked your ass!") were replaced with lyrics or tongue-in-cheek pronouncements which would only make sense to insiders (as an extreme example, the back of one Nirvana shirt reads "Flower sniffin/Kitty pettin/Baby kissin/Corporate rock whores"). As a trend, '90s irony replaced '80s

ck Tees in the 1990s

Unfortunately, such wit did not also ensure great imagery. With few exceptions, the improvements in printing technology which had spurred design innovation throughout the '70s and '80s began detracting from rock T-shirts' appeal by the early '90s. Computers allowed for unprecedented levels of detail in the prints, as well as an impressive range and subtlety in colors, but manufacturers chose to showcase the realism possible with the new technology rather than explore engaging designs. Likewise, in keeping with the anti-glitz stance of many of the groups, decorative gimmicks used to enhance T-shirts in past decades became non-existent: '90s shirts have no glitter, no glow-in-the-dark ink, no contrasting ribbing. As a result of these changes, most rock shirts made during the '90s lack the personality and intimacy of tees from the previous two decades. Largely uncreative, '90s shirts feel influenced by corporate decisions, not rock and roll.

To be fair, rock tees had spent nearly twenty years at the top of the coolest clothing heap. Yet fashion, like all arts, is a cycle; tastes change, looks come and go, eventually even the most beloved basics go out of style for a while. Once a trend's popularity has peaked, there is an inevitable fall from grace. Even icons like jeans and sneakers have gone through dark periods when they were less than cool. After two decades as the ultimate insider fashion statement (by any standard, an incredibly long run), rock T-shirts were due for a fall out.

And by the mid '90s, the golden years of rock T-shirts were over.

This amateur bootleg for the Clash of the Titans tour features classic heavy metal images, riffing on recognizable Megadeth T-shirt graphics. They suddenly look out of place next to the newer T-shirt designs of up-and-coming '90s artists.

Clash of the Titans Tour *1990*

Many late-'80s–early-'90s metal bands just printed high-resolution copies of album covers shown large across the front of their tees; that is the case with this shirt for Warrant, one of the last metal bands to score major success. Though the shirt doesn't look bad, it certainly lacks the energy and individuality of earlier rock tees.

Warrant *1990*

Many indie and alt-rock bands recognized the homogeneity of the mainstream metal audience and distanced themselves from it through greater community and world awareness. That comes across in this tee for perennial favorites the Violent Femmes, which has graphics designed with a decidedly ethnic flair.

Violent Femmes *1990*

Mudhoney was an anti-glam band out of the northwest. This tee is like many from '90s grunge and indie artists in that it rejects self-aggrandizing graphics for an ironic, obscure image. Again, there is nothing about the shirt which would suggest that Mudhoney is a band. Many artists in the '90s were consciously positioning themselves against the standards and expectations of mainstream rock.

Mudhoney ca. *1990*

The Creatures *1990*

One innovation in '90s rock tee design was the giant front print, with no band name. These shirts for the Creatures (fronted by Siouxsie Sioux of Siouxsie and the Banshees) and the Cult (above) can only be identified as rock shirts by the group names which are printed on the back.

The Cult *ca. 1991*

Guns N' Roses was one of the biggest bands of the '80s, and they remained superstars when they released *Use Your Illusion*, a two-disk effort, in the early '90s. This tee features images that are totally '80s—the skull and pistols—on a totally '90s shirt of oversized, heavy cotton.

Gun N' Roses *1991*

Alice in Chains was one of the most successful grunge bands, with an incredibly heavy, grinding sound totally unlike the glam metal which preceded them. Consequently, it is no surprise that this T-shirt looks little like earlier rock tees. Drab colors and an all-over pattern are nothing like the center-framed graphics of decades past. Perhaps the only visual indication that Alice in Chains is a heavy rock band comes across in the odd, isolated illustrations of body parts—a spine, an eyeball—which hearken to the classic images of bands like Megadeth.

Alice in Chains *1991*

An example of a more mainstream, early '90s rock shirt look from which alternative artists were distancing themselves.

Damn Yankees *1992*

Hole ca. *1991*

Unlike the shirts from the previous two decades, tees in the '90s were increasingly likely to sport only a band's name. These shirts could be mass-produced at little cost (no designers to pay if only an established logo was picked up), but it is easy to see why these T-shirts are the least popular among vintage rock shirt collectors today.

Smashing Pumpkins *ca. 1993*

Classic rock imagery still worked on T-shirts for heavy rock bands like Motörhead which had never had a glamorous or MTV-friendly style.

Motörhead *1992*

A '90s take on the festival T-shirt, this tee, from the second Lollapalooza Festival, features cleaner graphics and minimal color, as well as a much roomier fit, compared to festival shirts from the previous two decades.

Lollapalooza Festival *1992*

Pearl Jam *ca. 1993*

Anti-glam T-shirts for grunge's biggest stars, Nirvana and Pearl Jam, show a clear divergence—the designs on these T-shirts are simple and unassuming. The Nirvana tees in particular reject rock's precedents: The back of the shirt (above left) reads "Fudge Packin/Crack Smokin/Satan Worshippin/Mother Fucker" while the back of the other (above right) says "Flower Sniffin/Kitty Pettin/Baby Kissin/Corporate Rock Whores."

Nirvana ca. 1993
Nirvana ca. 1993

Sonic Youth ca. 1994

Rejecting the archetypal rock T-shirt style, many shirts for alternative artists featured graphics inspired by other commercial art styles, such as comic books and vintage movie posters.

The Melvins *ca. 1993*

Mark Arm

Mark Arm changed the way the world sees Seattle.

Well, maybe not directly, but as one of the leading, innovative musicians who pioneered the intense punk-metal northwest sound that came to be known as "grunge," Arm certainly played an integral role in the counterculture music scene that put Seattle on the world map in the early '90s. With a deviant fashion sense, a keen wit, and an exceptional wail, Arm was a driving force in seminal bands Green River (Stone Gossard and Jeff Ament were also members, in their pre-Pearl Jam days) and Mudhoney (the group he fronts to this day). He was also one of the first artists signed to the now-legendary Sub Pop label. As an artist and performer, Mark Arm was at the vortex of a musical maelstrom.

But, before it all, he was printing rock tees in a high school art class.

Recalls Arm, "The first rock T-shirt that I had was one that I made myself in silkscreening class in high school and it was a Rush T-shirt. . . . That went out the window when punk rock came around." As a teenager in the late '70s and early '80s, Arm grew up not just with rock culture, but with rock tee culture, too. It was a time when, if you were a little creative and couldn't buy an official T-shirt (and unless you attended the concert, opportunities to buy a particular band's tee were slim), you made one yourself. Later, after graduating high school, Arm found a shop which would reprint designs onto T-shirts using a newfangled Xerox technology; he used the discovery to print up shirts for favorite "underground" artists such as Black Flag and Crass.

This was a time when wearing the right rock tee really said something. As Arm says, rock T-shirts in high school were, "totally a social signifier." With his noteworthy sense of humor, Arm continues, "You saw someone with a Styx T-shirt, you knew to stay away from them." He adds that, conversely, "especially in the late '70s, if you saw anybody wearing a punk rock or new wave shirt it was definitely a signifier. . . . Battle lines were being drawn. . . . I mean, if you saw some guy with a Devo shirt, even if he looked like a hippie, you knew that guy was definitely cooler than the guy in the Led Zeppelin shirt."

Yet Arm never became deeply concerned with T-shirts for his own bands. For instance, mid-'80s Seattle superstars Green River are largely regarded as radical music innovators; they were a major force in the Northwest scene. But despite Arm's awareness of rock tees as a youth, rock T-shirts were not a big deal for the band. This is not to say that Green River tees were not important; just ask any Seattle scenester from back in the day and they'll likely recall a Green River T-shirt as a regular feature in any cool Seattleite's wardrobe. That said, Arm contends that the band's sometimes irreverent shirts were something of an afterthought: "I think that, more than anything, we were trying to amuse ourselves."

Mudhoney, Arm's next major music group, followed a similar track. Though Mudhoney achieved significant national and international renown by the early '90s, their singer claims, "We've never been good at marketing and merchandising ourselves." T-shirts for the band certainly exist; indeed, on several tours they had merchandising managers whose sole responsibility was the sale of band-related products. And Arm has kept at least one example of every Mudhoney T-shirt ever made. Yet he would be at a loss to tell you just how much money Mudhoney has made from T-shirt sales, or the specific impetus for almost any given tee design.

What Arm does remember is trading band tees with other groups while on tour. "Playing shows around the country," he says, "there'd be the inevitable end of show T-shirt swap. . . . We'll trade you four of ours for four of yours kind of thing." Today, his attic is filled with rock tees collected in this manner. One of his favorite shirts is a Radio Birdman tee given to him by Deniz Tek while they were touring together in the DKT/MC5 a few years back. It seems that for Arm, even after achieving rock stardom, rock tees are still in the realm of the fan. And as a musician respected for his down-to-earth personality almost as much as his creativity and talent, he still appreciates T-shirts of his favorite artists. In fact, after all these years, he's still looking for the perfect Stooges shirt.

Billion-Dollar Babies: The Rep

Sometime around the turn of the millennium, interest in vintage rock T-shirts surged. Suddenly, the ratty old shirts for yesteryear's favorite bands were hot again. These tees that had been the height of coolness, then the ultimate sign of loserdom, had come full circle. Reworked vintage rock tees—shirts that were restyled, or embellished with rhinestones, grommets, and other such doodads—were très chic in the late '90s, but that wasn't quite the same thing. Those tees were one-of-a-kind pieces worked over by crafty hipster artisans. The new century's crush on vintage rock T-shirts was for the real deal—shirts that hadn't been reinterpreted. The well-dressed were jonesing for rock-and-roll authenticity.

Six years later, what looked to be a flash-in-the-pan trend is still with us. Vintage rock shirts, like those featured herein, command top dollar across the country and on eBay. Yet their mass appeal and limited availability moved prices beyond the average consumer's clutches. So, savvy entrepreneurs once again saw an opportunity in the rock T-shirt market and a new industry was born: reproduction rock T-shirts.

Some streetwise businesspeople recognized that the public wasn't just clamoring for T-shirts with band logos; the right name on a regular tee didn't make a shirt popular. (And, of course, it never had.) Slapping "AC/DC" on a Hanes Beefy XXL T-shirt simply didn't cut it. No. What people were responding to were the vintage rock-and-roll graphics on the old shirts! So rock merchandise companies such as Chaser, Signatures, and Trunk began printing up new T-shirts for old bands, reproducing vintage graphics on tees styled for a classic retro fit. The results were rock tees which had the look of vintage, but the price tag of new. Rock T-shirts were cool again, and the increased availability and affordability of the reproduction shirts only spurred the market.

Of course, some devout rock-and-rollers—purists, we'll call them—continue to bemoan the widespread sale of vintage-style rock tees. And they are doubly put out by that strange twist within the phenomenon, wherein many artists who never had T-shirts in their heyday now have licensed reproductions—shirts meant to look like tees that never actually existed.

(It's a post-modern paradox that we'll let sociology students unravel.) These purists don't like the idea of people co-opting cult artists in an attempt at instant street cred. They cringe at the thought of rock tees in chain stores. Music is art, not fashion, right?

But consider this from another angle: If you love a band, why should you be forced to choose between wearing a less cool, generic shirt and ponying up hundreds of dollars for vintage authenticity? The fact is, rock and roll is timeless and many of the great artists are more popular today than they were way back when. There simply aren't enough vintage rock tees to go around. The reproduction rock T-shirt industry has let legions of new fans in on the action.

What's more, bands actually make money on the sale of reproduction tees, which are licensed, as opposed to the resale of vintage tees (technically referred to as "after market" sales) for which they get nothing. Of course, this is not to suggest that artists are making a mint on the sale of reproduction rock tees. Few are. But if you appreciate someone's music and the sale of reproduction shirts gives them a cash infusion, helping to extend their career, is that such a bad thing? And those folks who wear rock tees just to look cool, without any affection for the music, are contributing to the cause, too. Every time someone dons a rock T-shirt, they become a public billboard and an artist is promoted. The true fans might roll their eyes at the reproduction rock tees, but that only reiterates that the social significance of the shirts hasn't changed: Wearing a great rock tee is still about being in the know, and reproduction rock shirts have only added a layer of subtlety to the message.

There was a time, thirty or so years ago, when rock T-shirts were new, incredible things. They let fans connect with their heroes in a radically intimate way. And they still do. The enduring popularity of rock tees testifies, in a way record sales never will, to the extreme connection people have with their favorite music and the continued appeal of rock iconography.

Just like great rock music, great rock T-shirts are timeless. Their look is classic, their designs resonate.

Rock and roll is here to stay. And so are rock tees.

MC5 2002

One of the most popular tees for MC5 put out by Chaser (opposite page) combines the group's classic logo with a vintage Detroit muscle car graphic to reflect their roots. During the band's first era of popularity in the 1960's, no original MC5 tees were ever produced. The band's bassist, Michael Davis, a former art student, now helps create many of the group's T-shirt designs, including this one. Another Chaser-produced shirt (above) incorporates iconic MC5 graphics on a thin, narrow-cut, vintage-style tee. This T-shirt can also be purchased without the potentially controversial upside-down marijuana leaf.

MC5 *2002*

The T-shirt that was worn by pop singer Justin Timberlake on the cover of *Vibe*.
Showcasing original MC5 artwork from a vintage concert poster, it features an American flag backdrop
that expounds on the band's ideas of freedom.

MC5 *2002*

This is the tee Jennifer Aniston sported on the hit sitcom *Friends*. Produced by Levi's relatively early in the new millennium's vintage rock tee revival, these high-quality T-shirts flaunt bold reproductions of some of the band's original graphics for faux-vintage authenticity.

MC5 *2002*

Wayne Kramer

For someone who doesn't wear printed T-shirts, Wayne Kramer's life has certainly been affected by them.

In 2003, the legendary guitarist received a call from a journalist wanting his opinion on the MC5 T-shirts being sold by Levi Strauss & Co. It was the first Kramer had heard about the fashion giant's plans to release a line of clothes inspired by his iconic, late-'60s band.

As it turned out, Levi's had licensed MC5 artwork from Gary Grimshaw, the artist who created much of the radical group's visual materials in the '60s. Unfortunately, while Grimshaw owned the rights to his art, he had no control over the MC5 logo. So, with the Levi's/MC5 clothing already in production, the band's surviving members—Kramer, Mike Davis, and Dennis Thompson—were left in a difficult situation. Their choices were to proceed working with the denim corporation or to pursue legal action (which was particularly unappealing because it would force their old friend, Grimshaw, to return the money Levi's had already paid him).

Ultimately, after careful research and consideration, Kramer says, "we made lemonade out of lemons." Levi's released a limited run of MC5 T-shirts and other clothing inspired by the legendary Detroit rock group. Grimshaw kept his payment. And the surviving members of the band, who had maintained only minimal contact for thirty years, regrouped to play a special concert in London with support from Levi's; the event was filmed for a live DVD release. It seemed as though everyone was benefiting from a potentially disastrous situation.

But then boy-bander Justin Timberlake was pictured on the cover of a hip-hop magazine wearing a Levi's-issue MC5 T-shirt, and sitcom star Jennifer Aniston was featured in an MC5 tee on an episode of *Friends*. Many fans of the group—infamous for its anarchic live shows and antiestablishment rhetoric as much as its music—balked; the message boards on Kramer's website (www.waynekramer.com) became forums of fierce debate. While some fans were amused by the mainstream's Johnny-come-lately acceptance of the band, many people vigorously trashed MC5 as sellouts; the naysayers did not join in Kramer's amusement at the situation, or his observation that the mass-media appearances of MC5 T-shirts were "the idea of the revolution that we were talking about [the politics championed by the group in the late '60s]. To use the machine against itself."

The story became one of the biggest music industry scandals of 2003, generating far more commentary (and, to be honest, wrath) than mainstream appropriation of songs by, for example, punk legend Iggy Pop—who licensed music to Royal Caribbean cruise lines, or rock icons Led Zeppelin—whose music appeared in Cadillac commercials. For a band that had never achieved great commercial success, and who had been largely out of the public eye for three decades, the sudden, intense attention was startling.

Respectful of others' opinions, Kramer let MC5 devotees hash things out on his site's message boards. As he puts it, "If people want to be critical and have opinions about it, it's perfectly all right with me. . . . If they want to think that MC5 is supposed to live up in the mountains and eat berries and come down and have guerrilla warfare in the streets, that's their fantasy." But, the reality is, as strongly as some people feel about the band, MC5 has yet to become fabulously wealthy off of their music. And they aren't becoming rich off of their T-shirts now.

The public's dramatic reaction to the MC5/Levi's deal and the subsequent appearance of the group's T-shirts on vanilla-grade celebrities underscores the extremely intimate feelings fans attach to rock tees, as well as the very delicate situation created by the reproduction rock T-shirt industry. For much of the rock audience, the fragile balance between art and commerce, support and exploitation, is quite hazy. They often regard any representation of their favorite artists as a sacred sign and something that should only be brandished among true believers. In the case of MC5, the band's counterculture legacy as the definitive revolutionary rock group and the forefathers of both punk and heavy metal make the issue particularly tense.

But as far as Kramer is concerned, the group never betrayed their radical reputation or liberal politics. They found a workable solution to an unpleasant situation, and that unpleasant situation ended up being the catalyst for the regrouping of MC5's living members. Today, Kramer, Davis, and Thompson perform around the world as DKT/MC5; in 2005 they played 100 concerts. (The original MC5 only played 300 in the whole five years they were together.) They have a selection of licensed reproduction rock shirts put out by Chaser (as a '60s band, MC5 predated the rock tee phenomenon; there are no original MC5 T-shirts); and Japanese fashion house Hysteric Glamour also released a line of clothes inspired by the group. And they each have a life outside of MC5.

"To succeed as an artist means, in my humble opinion, to continue to create," says Kramer. "Artists don't live in castles; they're not funded by the church or state," he continues. "We're funded by our own efforts. So, if I can sell a T-shirt and that helps me pay my rent and I can continue . . . there's no downside to that."

Our sincere thanks to these exceptional folks....

For their early support: James Babyteeth, Pony Maurice, Lynette Krall, Dhany Reed, Gordon Raphael, Ben Ireland, Stormy, Allen Arkush, Ralph Saenz, Elliot Siegel, Adam Mandel, Jane Kloecker, Jacob Anderson, Dorian Toop, A.J. DeLange, Jade Harris, Helen Harlan.

For their generous assistance and contributions: Pamela des Barres, Tommy Ramone, Paul Kallish, Danny Fields, Vern Evans, Roberta Bayley, Angela and Mike Davis, Margaret and Wayne Kramer, Richard Hell, Mark Arm, and Arturo Vega.

And, for making it all happen: Donna Gaines—an inspiration and catalyst; Susan Ramer—an unparalleled champion; and Tamar Brazis—the one who pulled all of this together.

We would like to acknowledge the following for the use of their rock tees: Jacob Anderson (Sex Pistols, page 38; L.A. Guns, page 129), A.J. DeLange (The Misfits, page 93), Jade Harris (Iggy Pop, page 38; Elvis Costello and the Attractions, page 81), Jane Kloecker (David Bowie, page 18; Lou Reed, page 18; The Rolling Stones, page 21), and Dorian Toop (King Diamond, page 151).